SINGLE WOMAN

Distributed by: Small Press Distribution (SPD), 1341 Seventh Street, Berkeley CA 94710; Ingram Periodicals Inc.,18 Ingram Blvd., LaVergne, TN 37086 and Ubiquity Distributors, Inc. 607 Degraw St., Brooklyn, NY 11217. Available also from Box Turtle Press.
ISBN: 978-1-893654-17-4

Cover painting: Mary Heilmann, "Violette", 1991. Image provided courtesy of the artist, 303 Gallery, and Hauser & Wirth, © Mary Heilmann
Book design: Anne Lawrence
Typeset in Futura Book

Publisher: Box Turtle Press
184 Franklin Street
New York, New York 10013
212.219.9278; mudfishmag@aol.com
www.mudfish.org

MUDFISH INDIVIDUAL POET SERIES # 10

SINGLE WOMAN

Poems by Dell Lemmon

CONTENTS

CONTENTS

CATS AND DOGS

Some people think my life is pathetic
and perhaps they are right.

I hang up the phone
after being cut off
by an old friend and I am alone
again in my house on Cape Cod
in early June.

Not completely alone – I have my
sixteen-year-old black lab, who
needs to be fed rice and chicken broth
with a little bit of wet dog food.

The house smells like pee,
which smells a little bit like popcorn –
salty and sweet at the same time.

I turn on the television for news and weather,
heat two pots of water – one to replenish
his supply of rice and one for my pasta.

The packaged Caesar salad with pre-washed
lettuce, creamy dressing, garlic croutons,
and parmesan cheese tastes surprisingly good.

There's a violin concerto playing on the radio
as the last light from a cloudy day slowly dims
between bright green leaves outside the windows.

Later, after taking my dog outside to pee
with no success as he seems to have stopped
peeing outside in the evenings,

I settle into bed with my poetry books.

I am grateful for the silence and opportunity
to read again Hayden Carruth's "Birthday Cake."
I have folded down the corner to that page.

He is grateful at age 70
to be in love with a woman
age 42 and to know that she
loves him.

At age 56, I am in love
with a man age 39,

but I don't lie in bed
with him the way Hayden
Carruth lies in bed with her.

I don't even speak to him
and I have never heard him
say my name.

Some people think that I am gay,
because I have lived alone for so long.

Certainly, I have always been ambivalent
about how females are supposed to act.

I know that because of my gender
and age, unlike Hayden Carruth,
I cannot assume that young man
loves me.

But I can love him,
as long as it stays hidden
like a wild cat in the night.

Suddenly, my sleeping dog
moves his feet and makes a noise
dreaming his doggy dreams.

ONE

THE SEWERS OF PARIS

I google the name of a little boy
I babysat in France. His mother
told me over 25 years ago that
he had an unusual and antiquated
French name so maybe I will find
him and sure enough he's on Facebook
and he has a lot of friends with French names,
which surprises me, because I always forget
about the two years I spent living in France.

I never even went to see the Eiffel Tower.
I used to take my visitors to *des egouts*.
I thought a boat ride through the sewers
was such a funny way to see Paris, or not,
and the smell was not too bad.
The only thing that made any sense
to me back then was reading
a biography of Janis Joplin titled
Buried Alive and writing letters
to my friend in Mexico. It was a relief
not to understand the language
that people were speaking around me.
I just sat in cafés, sipping coffee,
and staring out the window.

Until I got the job taking care
of a little boy who acted like an older man.
Soon it was clear that he was taking care

of me. I never had any idea where
we were and he knew the names of all
the subway stops at age three.
Il est tres intelligent, the old lady
sitting beside us declared loudly.
I used to ask him to translate words.
"What is it when there is something
in the air and you cannot see clearly?"
Brume, Dell, ca c'est brume!
he answered brusquely as if I was a student
who had not done her homework
and should know the word for fog,
even if I was lost in a fog, especially
if I was as lost as I was.

Once when we were eating fish,
he suddenly blurted out, *Des Arêtes!*
Attention, Dell, attention!
He was warning me not to choke
on bones. *Toi, aussi,* I answered
weakly. I used to tell him stories
to pass the time and prepare him
for all the lies he would encounter
as an adult. I was recovering from some
of those lies as I hid out in Paris. Once,
when we were walking down the Champs Elysees
after swimming in a public pool, he asked me
to carry him. "No, my arms are broken," I replied
and showed him the break at my elbows.
Dell, tu fais des histoires encore, he responded
in a weary voice. At least he didn't call me
a liar, only a fabricator of tales.

I heard his mother screaming as I lay
on the bed in my attic room. She had just
discovered that her husband was having an affair
with her best friend. I listened tensely until
his favorite grandfather burst through the front door
calling out his name. *Arnaud! Arnaud!*
"Papi!" he shrieked in agony and relief.
I had to pick him up at nursery school
the next day and he was sitting all alone
in a corner with a big frown on his face.
Je veux voir Papi, he stated firmly
when he saw me. "Papi isn't here.
Only Dell." He thought for a moment
and then followed me out the door.

I took him home to listen to Janis Joplin.
We turned the music up high and
chased each other around the furniture
laughing and screaming
louder than Janis.

HEART BREAK RHYME

35 years after
I was found
wandering around

a field in Marlboro,
I drive over a hill
in Vermont and

pass a turn-off
to Marlboro
on my way

to a writing workshop
in Wilmington. So after
I find the workshop,

I turn around, as if
still wandering, and
drive back to Marlboro.

There's an old graveyard
by the turn-off
with flat, gray stones

slanting in the dusk
and autumnal colors
burning all around.

I drive down
the country road
to the country college

in the beautiful hills,
where a Holocaust survivor
started a music festival

in 1951. In 1979,
I arrived in a taxi
after taking a bus

because I had to see
the person who broke
my heart one more time.

I also wanted
to see the place
he loved so well

where he spent summers
as a child while
his father played

the violin.
It all looks
so harmless now,

so quiet, so serene,
so undisturbed. Back then,
I was so disturbed

by its beauty,
by his beauty,
by the beauty

of the violin playing
world, while I was a
WASP from the suburbs

who only listened to
rock and roll
and pop. Who knew

a Jew from
New York could
love me?

Who knew
I could be so blue
when he stopped?

I got out of the taxi,
asked for him
at the box office,

and then started
wandering around
the green hills

until he found me
and called out my name
in despair because

he didn't want me
there. I was expunged
forever without him

after I had absorbed
him through my skin,
which was thin anyway,

and then the sounds
of that violin like
stranded sea nymph

sirens singing
thru the walls –
their seductive calls.

It's really not fair
at all – how I fell
in love the first time.

I was so unprepared –
so scared, so barely there –
so sure I would fall

apart and I did.
But 35 years later,
I drive over a hill –

35 years after
I was found
wandering around.

ANTI-POSTCARDS

My grandmother
collected postcards
when she was young.

I died
when she was young.

I lied.
I grew up
and she

died when
I was young.

I cried
when I was
young

and old
and no one
ever told

why she died
so young.

I have
the postcards
she collected.

Hundreds of
black and white
photographs

of Europe
decimated
after World War I

One site / sight
after the next
bombed to oblivion

Who sent
those postcards
to whom
and why?

And how is it
now the world
has been pieced
back together,

but my grandmother's
anti-postcards
look so contemporary

like the future
rather than
the past.

I died
when she was young.

THERE'S SOMETHING TO BE SAID FOR SUICIDE

(To Vijay Seshadri)

A poet told me
that he likes to read
the suicide poets,
even though
he has never
been suicidal
himself. There is
something to be said
for suicide,
or at least,
the possibility of it.

I grew up with suicide
and what it always meant
to me
was that you could walk away.
You did not have to take
what was dished onto your plate.
It can also be
a creative force
that compels you
to do things differently,
because you need
something else
in order to keep living.

One of my favorite suicides,
Spalding Gray,
used to interview audience
members at his performances.
One time I saw him
grilling a young guy
who worked as a fireman
in downtown Manhattan.
Spalding wanted to know
whether he was a suicidal pyromaniac
and if that was the real reason
he was a fireman.
The guy answered as honestly
as I have ever seen anyone
answer a question. "I saved
a life
when I was eighteen years old
and I never
got over the high.
Sure, some guys
are suicidal,
but no one puts them
in charge,
and you always want them
on your team because

they will go into a fire
to save a life
when no one else will."

I will always remember Spalding
for the fearless way
he discarded form and tradition
in the theater in order
to create
something different.
And I will also always
remember that fireman
for his honesty,
his intellectual curiosity –
attending such esoteric,
avant-garde performance art
after a day at the firehouse,
and for his bravery.

Just as there is something to be said
for suicide, there is much
to be said against it.
I worry that because that fireman
worked in downtown Manhattan,
he went into a fire
caused by suicidal fanatics
flying some planes
from which there could be

no return.

WALKING BACK

Christmas, 1982. How I walked to the end of the world
before deciding to walk back, how I arrived
at a deserted train station in a boarded up
beach town outside of Barcelona, and a taxi
picked me up and dropped me off
at the only hotel open for business
filled with a busload of retired Germans.

I saw the way they looked at food that night
and realized that they had gone without,
and realized that they had lived through
World War II and I had not. I was a lone,
lost, young American woman, but they accepted
me at their table to share food anyway. One
of them even gave me a Christmas gift.

She said that she had a daughter back in Germany
and I remembered that I had a mother somewhere.
And after spending a few days lying on
the beach in a winter coat, splashing in cold water,
and drinking coffee at sunset with a group of tourists
who had lived through World War II, I decided
to live too. If they could keep living

after that, so could I after this.
And thirty years later, I wrote down the story

of that Christmas and then I made dinner
and ate too much, as I generally do these days,
and walked my dog at sunset. When I got back,
rather than turn on my computer again, I picked
up a pen to write down a poem on paper.

I am in love with a young man.
I am an old man in love with a beautiful woman.
I am a young dog in love with his boy.
I am a young girl in love with freedom.
I am an overweight, middle-aged woman
in love with
a fantasy.

Like the sunset,
he makes everything shine
in a seductive glow
so that I want to live
with a ravenous hunger
that I never knew
in my dark youth.

ON OVERCOMING OBSTACLES

Virginia Woolf could not cross a puddle.
It is well documented. Just google
Virginia Woolf and puddle.

She came to the puddle.
She could not cross it.
She was suspended.
"Identity failed me," she wrote.
"We are nothing," she thought.
And then she forced herself
to cross the puddle
and put her hand
against a brick wall
to bring herself
back into her body.

I have thought of that moment
often– how easily
you can be thrown off course,
how suddenly it can all seem
like a thin veneer, masking
a big, black hole.

But then you push on.
You persevere

past those moments.
You forget about
death and the vast constellations
hidden behind the thin blue sky.
You focus
on the task at hand –
getting across a puddle
so that you can buy
flowers for a dinner party
with friends.

TWO

FAMOUS AND NOT

The other night I turned on
the television right
where the movie *The Godfather*
gets interesting.
Al and Diane are sitting
across the table from one another
and he gets up to go. And she asks,
"When will I see you again?"

Watching the film again,
late at night in middle age,
I remembered how the culture
of my youth was enthralled
by Mario Puzo's book,
Francis Ford Coppola's movie,
and Al Pacino's acting.
I completely ignored the film
in 1972. But then
I went to theater school

and Charlie spent all day
in between classes
acting out scenes
as Al Pacino in *Dog Day Afternoon*.
And David directed Al
in *Richard III* on Broadway
and Laura acted in it
and I went to see the production

in Philadelphia and afterwards
sat at a long table with
Al sitting at the head of it
like the king in the play.

I just saw Al again
in *Merchant of Venice*. And
I googled David afterwards
because I wondered what
had happened to him. He discovered
so many great actors.
He had them all listed
in his little black book:
Al, Bobby Duval, Bobby De Niro.
And like some bad movie plot
when I googled David,
I found out that a guy
brought his friend and film script
to David's class at Harvard.
And at a recent benefit gala,
they, meaning Matt Damon and Ben Affleck,
said that David was the whole reason
they were there.

And then I heard from Laura
that David had died.
It's weird how someone
can live and die and affect
the lives of everyone in the room,
but only a select group of people
knows that person's name and yet
so many people know the names

of Matt Damon, Ben Affleck,
Al Pacino, Dustin Hoffman,
Robert De Niro, and we will
be watching them in films
for years to come.

Al said that
they should put up
a statue of David.

CHARLIE ON YOUTUBE

Last night I took the subway
out to Brooklyn during rush hour
to meet with five other poets
in a small, overheated room.
This morning I clicked on YouTube
to watch Charlie walk onstage
after a film critic called him the most
creative screenwriter of his generation.
Five poets sitting in a room versus
a standing ovation in an auditorium –
I sort of prefer the poets,
but maybe that's my problem.

I never dreamed of success.
I liked travelling on the road
to somewhere different, with other
creative misfits. I liked asking
the big questions, looking
for answers, going to coffee shops.
Charlie liked coffee shops too.
We went to a lot of them
together. I even worked in one
and he came to visit me there
and drew cartoons on the napkins.
Charlie can really draw. A lot
of people don't know that.

This summer, I emailed him
a photo of me on the beach

and asked him to email me
a photo of his ten-year old daughter
whom I had not seen since she
was a toddler. And he sent one
back right away from his i-Phone.
They were having breakfast at
a coffee shop. She was not smiling
and had not finished her eggs.
And when I emailed that
I was having a summer romance
with poetry, Charlie asked me
which poets I liked, but he did
not respond when I asked him
which poets he liked.
It's hard for me to grasp

the larger picture. It's hard
for me to understand how many
people know him now. It's
as if they all gained a friend
when I lost one. He never
calls me when he comes
to New York, even though I am
in almost all of his movies. Sometimes
I can tell from reading the reviews before
seeing the film, which character is me.
The lonely one that got away. I remember
the shock I felt the first time
I saw myself on the screen. Charlie's
character says *I love you*, and I say

I love you too, Charlie! – although
Charlie denies that he was thinking
of me when he wrote those scenes.
But what about the name of Kate
Winslet's character in "Eternal
Sunshine of the Spotless Mind"
and my name? Clementine and
Lemmon. They even call her
Tangerine at one point.

He can deny it as much as he wants,
but when I kept pressing him
about it on the phone, Charlie did
acknowledge one thing. *I think
I've told you this before*, he said
in his soft-spoken, measured way,
*You were the first person I was
passionate about. You are etched
onto my being.*

I am etched onto his being.

And I am in those films.
And he is in this poem,
which I will read to five
other poets in Brooklyn.

BEING FEMALE

In high school, there was this boy, who called me on the telephone to talk for hours and imitated me at parties relentlessly. I met people who said, "You're the girl Jim B– imitates."

I told my mother that I couldn't do my homework, because this guy wouldn't stop talking to me on the telephone.

"You can't be mean to boys," was her only response.

Years later, a shrink said that it could have been a case of sexual harassment.

The Christmas before 9/11 as my father was dying, I received a holiday letter from Jim, who had married, had two kids, published a few books, and gotten tenured. He told the story of his son swallowing a marble by accident and waiting for the marble to pass through his digestive system. When it did, the marble came out a different color and his son exclaimed, "It's a Christmas Miracle!"

Jim then proceeded to use the marble incident as a metaphor for his own miraculous transformation. I had noticed that the return address spelled out Jennifer rather than Jim, but Jim had always confused me, so I figured he was making a weird joke.

In April, I opened a letter from Jennifer with photographs and a detailed account of her sex change.

Shortly after 9/11, I received a copy of her memoir, She's Not There with a note saying she had appeared on the Oprah Show and asking me if I was aware of all these events.

I sent back a postcard saying that I was glad everything worked out so well, but I was overwhelmed at the moment by 9/11 and the death of my father.

Shortly afterwards, a journalist friend of mine interviewed Jennifer about her memoir. When he mentioned my name, Jennifer responded, "Oh, she's the girl I always wanted to be!"

My mother has been dead for years and I regret that I cannot tell her that he's not a boy anymore.

So does that mean I can be mean to her now?

DRAG QUEENS

You talked
about drag queens
in yoga, as if the class
didn't know about
drag queens.

Yesterday, in the Egyptian
section of the museum,
I stood in front of
a small, clay female figure
with no breasts and
her face obscured.

The art history
lecturer didn't like
the boring sphinxes,
so he took us to a more
sensual section
of Egyptian art,

where everything
flickered alive
for a few seconds,
highlighting the human
desire to escape
into a world of objects,
where the unreal

seems more real
than the real.

The sculpted crowds
on those clay tablets
came alive
like a scene
in a film.

That night, I went to
the opening at MOMA
for Cindy Sherman's show.
Tom wanted to skip
the cocktail party and
go straight to the art.
He liked the black and white
film stills best,
while I felt a particular
fondness for the grotesque
nude women with obscene
prosthetics.

Tom and I had dinner
at China Grill afterwards.
And then I went to yoga class
the next day and you
were talking about drag queens
as if I had not had dinner
with Happy Phace and Taboo!
in their East Village apartment
during the 1980s when
drag queens were still taboo

and Taboo!'s paintings
were covered in glitter.

And now all the kids
watch television shows
starring drag queens.

HISTORY / NO HISTORY

I didn't want to go to the panel with the famous, handsome, male poet / memoirist.

It was snowing in Boston.

I was staying in a small, elegant hotel two blocks away from where I lived as an undergraduate at Boston University.

Back then I woke up during a snowstorm to discover that the parking meters had almost disappeared under snow.

I figured that the famous, handsome, male poet / memoirist wouldn't see me in the large crowd and even if he did, he wouldn't recognize or know me.

I trudged down the hallway at the convention center in my heavy boots and coat with a weird knitted headband holding back messy hair and a dirty, ragged scarf wrapped around my neck and big eye glasses, wet with melted snow.

When I looked up, he was staring directly at me, as if he was fully exposed, as if he had no clothes on, as if he was that beautiful, and there was no one between us.

Men are like dogs. They never forget.

I passed him once – years ago – before he was famous, before he had married, before he had had a child...

I passed him once and paused – thinking maybe he was cute, thinking he was friends with most of the friends I had in that small town, thinking maybe I should say something.

But then there was something in his response to my pause that gave me pause,

and so I moved on – the way I usually do.

I could never figure out how a feminist could have sex with a man given the history of oppression of women by men – a history that so few people seemed to acknowledge or understand. History / no history.

People usually concluded that I was a fearful, self-loathing lesbian. Why they didn't think I was a fearful, self-hating hetero, I don't know. They couldn't seem to fathom the concept that the way the patriarchy saturated everything completely paralyzed me.

My mother was raped at 16, or at least that's what my brother told me. History /no history.

So then he became successful at writing memoirs (and I was desperately try-ing to write memoirs at the time) and he married a famous actress (and I had gone to acting school), who had played a famous feminist (and I am a femi-nist), and Hollywood made a movie out of one of his memoirs.

We had never actually had a conversation. (History / no history.) Once, one of my friends had invited him and his wife to a dinner party with a few other glamorous people and then my friend had invited me at the last minute, because I was not glamorous, but I already had plans.

When I checked out of the small, elegant hotel the morning after the panel, the snow had stopped and the streets were clear. I regretted that I had not walked in the direction of the dorm where I used to live.

That night alone in my bed with my old dog sleeping nearby, I watched Tony Kushner on PBS talk about writing the screenplay for "Lincoln."

He seemed to have great compassion and understanding for Mary Todd Lincoln.

I heard that with the money he made from working on that film, Tony Kushner had bought a second home in the small town where once I passed the famous poet / memoirist.

My mother was raped at 16 and I hate you.

PSALM OF SADNESS

I keep glancing
at the taxi driver's face
in the rear view mirror
thinking he is so handsome
why does he have such sad eyes?

I just wandered through
the art carnivals
in the shadow of death,
remembering the missing,
loving the gaping hole
in the thick, pink paint,
the portrait of an interracial couple
painted in 1958, the potatoes
pinned to the wall with red dots
next to them. They made me laugh –
those potatoes. And then
I walked out onto the street
and into a bookstore instead.
I bought a book, but even the book
reminded me of the past.
Everything was pulling me back,
bringing me down, making me feel
so inconsequential.

So I got into the cab
to go to an opening in SoHo
where I felt pretty sure

they would ignore me.
I had refused their request
to loan a photograph to the exhibition,
because I was tired of the hassle
and interruptions, the rude and arrogant
behavior, the damaged
or destroyed art work
when it was finally returned.

They had a big preview party
at The Four Seasons uptown and
as so often happens in the art world,
all the wrong people were invited.
All the people who actually knew
the artist and supported his work
when no one else would, like me,
were not invited.

We watched him die
a horrible death because
the deaths were horrible
back then. You saw them dying
in the streets. You saw it in their faces
but ignored the fact. You saw them buying
groceries at the corner store. You saw
their sunken cheeks, ashen skin, and skinny limbs.
You feared for your life and the lives of your friends,
but you were too young to express that fear.

The artist practically crawled to his last opening
at a gallery on the far side of the East Village.

He wanted a show at MOMA, but his dealer
could barely sell any of his work. (And now
there is a catalogue the size of a dictionary
with shows featuring his art planned for
around the world.) Back then, he died
in a hospital where the nurses
were afraid to go near the patients.
Suddenly, he was gone,
and so were his friends,
and other artists who had AIDS,
and then his dealer, and her husband too.
It was like living through a war
that they don't teach in high school
and no one remembers.

And twenty years later,
I take a cab
to the artist's opening in SoHo,
alone, remembering the missing,
because they are impossible
to forget, looking at the sad eyes
of the handsome cab driver
in the rear view mirror
and wondering what is
his sadness and what is mine?
And how are they mixing
together in the middle
of this mad and messy,
sad and sexy city?

ONE SUICIDE ENGAGES WITH ANOTHER

I went to the Whitney thinking I was going to see Tom Thayer's performance, but then I looked into the projection room and got sucked into the darkness to watch the end of a video by Mike Kelley.

It was all people and places in downtown Detroit. In between those scenes was footage of a replica of Mike Kelley's childhood home on the back of a flat bed truck travelling down Michigan Avenue, past strip clubs and motels, with a simple, rock and roll road song playing in the background.

I felt a little the way I felt the first time I saw Mike Kelley's work at the end of the 1980s. He had assembled some dirty, stuffed animals and burnt candles on the floor with a big, old quilt hanging on the wall and I thought, "What the fuck is this? It's sooo good!"

After the video ended, it took the Whitney people a while to set up for the lecture and discussion of Mike Kelley's work. The art historian had some kind of accent and he talked about Mike Kelley's work in terms of darkness and light, which seemed so banal and predictable.

But I was happy to hear him talk about institutional critique, because I had never thought of Mike Kelley's work that way, and I should have.

It was kind of devastating to be sitting there, hearing about the work, with everybody acting so normally, and knowing that Mike Kelley was gone.

Suicide is weird that way – how it makes everybody who is still alive look like a fool.

On the way back to my apartment, there was a woman sitting next to me at the front of the bus with a cane and a book in her hand. I noticed an old photograph of the Dakota apartment building on the back of her book, but I didn't think much of it because the woman seemed so disoriented. She kept asking what was the next stop and if this was the east side or the west side.

Finally, the bus pulled up in front of the Dakota and the woman with the book hobbled down to the sidewalk and stood smiling at the Dakota as the bus pulled away. Who knows what that story was about, but all I could think was,

Mike Kelley – how could you leave all this? How could you make that film documenting the beauty of all this and not see it? How could you think that film was a failure? (Because that's what they said at the lecture.) How could you succumb to the darkness when there is so much light? Detroit looks like our Parthenon – a magnificent ruin marking a lost culture. Mike Kelley – how could you?

The truth is that I knew perfectly well how he could do it because I had almost done it myself three decades ago. And now this great artist, who was about the same age as me, had fallen in the banal, predictable, same old, same old battle of

darkness against light.

I wanted to cry, but Mike Kelley would not have cried.

When she introduced the speakers after the video, Elizabeth Sussman, who gave Mike Kelley his first show at the Whitney in 1993 and got Mike Kelley to submit what would be his final work to the 2012 Biennial, said that losing Mike Kelley was the saddest thing she had ever endured.

And she said it with a smile.

THREE

I WANT MY SKIN BACK

I wrote a letter
to an actor
I do not know.
I saw him in a show,
but the show was long,
and I had to go.

I am getting old.
I send random
letters to people
I do not know.

I do not know
what color
my hair is.
I can barely see
without the glasses
I never wore
before.
And I want my skin
back.
I went in for a facial
and they gave me
an acid peel without
really explaining
that I would lose
a layer of skin.

I saw Colin's face
flicker across the face
of that charming publisher,
who also received one
of my random communications.
It was one of the sweetest
moments in my life,
because when someone dies
you assume
that you will never
see them again
and then for him
to be resurrected
in that tiny room
with such a fresh face
in such a fine suit.

That publisher
was so positive
in the face of such
overwhelming odds,
so determined
to publish books
no matter what
the obstacles.

My father always wanted to sell books.
He loved them
even though he didn't necessarily
understand them.

He loved them as objects,
almost like a fetish,
as if they were portals
into a world
he wanted to inhabit,
but felt unworthy
of inhabiting.
I think it was a class thing
from way back
when our ancestors
were farmers and books
were the only way out.

The publisher started a blog
where I read
that he played basketball
in college. In high school,
my father was a basketball star
and he got recruited by
the snobby, local prep school
to play on their basketball team.
I suspect that they
gave him a scholarship
but I am not sure.
In college, he met another
rich kid and married her.
He had a lot of charm,
as did Colin,
as did the publisher,
as did the actor who
I do not know.

The actor recited
almost the entire text of
The Great Gatsby.

My father never mentioned
basketball to any of his children
and I never saw Colin's mother
until she showed up at his memorial.

And I am passing too,
a rich kid who had a poor parent
pretending to be someone
I am not,
with fake hair
and one less
layer of skin.

So we beat on,
boats against the current,
borne back ceaselessly
into the past.

I sent an email to the publisher
in response to his blog.

I wrote a letter to an actor
I do not know.

BAUHAUS AND BEYOND

How my mother loved that
Bauhaus furniture, and how I
hated it. Everybody else had wooden

furniture and I couldn't understand
why we had to have plastic.
I couldn't understand why

my mother dressed like Cher
and sent a taxicab to pick me up.
I couldn't understand why

she learned to fly airplanes and
raced them across the country.
One weekend when I was about 12,

my family flew to New Hampshire
in a small Beechcraft piloted by
my mother and a co-pilot. Two days

later we all packed back into the plane
and taxied down the runway piled
high with snow on either side so that

the runway felt like a tunnel, a birth
canal into the beyond. I looked down
at the patterns of isolated strings of light.

Then I looked up at the abundant
sprays of stars above, layer upon
layer, and I wanted to go there.

I wanted to go there, but felt myself
caught in the darkness in between,
doomed to descend back down

to the lonely patterns below and
I didn't want to. So I started sobbing
as that little plane plowed through the

night, and my mother didn't understand
why I was sobbing. But it was as if I had
been stricken and there was nothing to say,

nothing to do. Who knows whose grief
possessed me in that little plane. Was it mine,
or my mother's? Or her mother's? (Who

nobody mentioned.) When I was a child,
I didn't understand. Now when I see that
furniture that I resented in museums,

I know that my mother was just trying
to be different. She was just trying to live
her life so that she didn't end up dying

like her mother, a possible suicide.
I just had to cry until that plane landed,
then we never spoke of the incident again.

READING: THE STORY OF MY CHILDHOOD

My parents
read all the time,
but never discussed
any of their reading
with each other
or anyone else, which
made reading seem
more like praying –
a silent conversation
with God.

My mother read
only best-selling
fiction – usually
romances,
and my father
read philosophy,
history of science,
historical fiction,
science fiction,
history, memoirs,
biographies, and
the newspaper.

My mother usually read
in the late afternoon
after she had finished
her chores that day

and before taking a
hot bath and changing
into a comfortable,
attractive outfit
for dinner with her
husband and children.
Elsa, who came
from Trinidad,
cooked the dinner
while my mother
read stretched out
on a cream-colored
chaise lounge
in her bedroom
by sliding glass doors
to the garden.

My father read
whenever he could –
waiting in lines,
flying on airplanes,
alone in hotel rooms
while traveling
on business,
lying on the beach
while vacationing
with family, or
even while driving
a car, he occasionally
glanced at a newspaper
in traffic.
When he retired,

he bought a mail
order, history
of science, used book
business from a professor
that he operated out
of the basement of
the home he shared
with his second wife.

I remember my father's
bewildered statement as
he was dying that
he could no longer
read. I think reading
was more important
to him than sports,
business, friendship, women,
his children, and God.
I never read
as a child –
only for homework
and the dreaded summer
reading list for school.
It wasn't until
both my parents
were dead that
I started reading
voraciously, as if
I was reading for
all three of us.

A SQUASH GAME AT THE RACQUET CLUB

My father and brother used to play squash together,
but I never went to see them. When I was younger,
I was too busy and as far as my life was concerned,
I wanted to get as far away from where they play
squash as I could. But in some ways, you never really
get away from where you were born. You carry that
place, those people, those memories, and that culture
with you until the day you die. So it has become an
annual ritual to return to this odd building on Park

Avenue between 52nd and 53rd to see my brother and
his son play squash in the National Father/Son Squash
Doubles Championship, but also to be reminded of
the extremely weird world into which I was born.
Just walking a few blocks on the Upper East Side
of Manhattan can remind me, but entering the epicenter
brings it home in the most dismal way. This time there
is a wedding and the bride's big dress almost blocks the
entrance. There are so many rules in this place such as

what to wear and I am not wearing it, but I know
what words to say, "Squash match," and the man
behind the desk responds, "Fourth floor." This is
the only building in Manhattan where there are 3
4th floors. In past years, I have made the mistake
of going to the first 4th floor, which is the men's
changing room. So this time, I know to push 4M

for the doubles squash courts and I can hear balls
bouncing off the walls as soon as the elevator

doors open. The match before the match when
my brother and nephew will play is still going on
and my brother and his eternally blonde wife are
sitting in the stands above the court watching.
My brother looks older but slightly more resigned
to the fact that I am his sister. It has taken over
50 years, and we both know that we are entering
the final stretch and we will die soon and the facts
probably aren't going to change between now and

then. We have known each other longer than we
have known almost anybody else. We have always
been at war, but we have also always been brother
and sister. We have witnessed each other's lives. One
of us will witness the other one die. I get bored with
the match before the one with my brother and nephew
so I get up to move around. My brother asks if I am
leaving already, because I have done things like that
in the past. This time I just want to find my nephews,

so I exit from the back of the stands to the stairs as
someone is blocking the entranceway. But I get stuck
in the stairs all the way to the basement. It seems that
this place also has several 1st floors and I can't figure
out which one is the lobby. On one of the first floors,
I pass a waiter, who tells me to take the service elevator
to the next floor, but when I exit the elevator, a guard

watching the security cameras tells me to go back up
the stairs where I find the waiter again, who looks at me

in disbelief. The security guard is not sure which door
leads to the lobby and these people act as if they have
never seen anyone from the other side in their territory.
This building has a twilight zone and I have entered it.
Eventually, I get back on the main elevator and go to
the men's changing room where I find my brother and
nephews. All three of them are over six feet tall. I tell
my brother that he has the brothers he always wanted
(instead of three sisters). I also tell him that my friend

couldn't come with me to watch squash, because
he is channeling entities. I have to repeat that
information a few times. "It's a Brazilian trance
dance. People come to ask questions to the entities,
which get channeled through other people, one of whom
is my friend." My brother has learned to stay very calm
no matter what happens in life – except on the squash
court. He takes squash very seriously and doesn't
smile once he enters the playing area. Today he plays

against a father who knew him in college when
he had a bad temper. This adversary knows that
my brother's Achilles' heel in squash is his temper,
so he is doing everything he can to make my brother
angry. He smiles and keeps getting in his way so that
my brother can't hit the ball. Even I know that this
isn't basketball and you are supposed to get out of the

way, but some people get confused or else deliberately
ignore the rules. It's getting tense because I know

my brother is angry about his opponent's sleazy
tactics and he really wants to beat this guy. I have
a bad temper too and I have to resist jumping up and
yelling, "You're making my brother angry!" Instead,
I marvel at how my nephew's hair reminds me of my
brother's hair when he was younger – thick and brown
with a slight hint of red – and how my brother's hair
is gray now, as our father's hair once was. I wonder what
kind of player our father was and how he passed along

his competitive spirit to his son. (My father was not one
of these very privileged people, so he must have loved
beating them at any game he could.) Now my brother
has passed along that same spirit to his sons. Luckily,
he did not pass on his bad temper and my nephew stays
extremely calm. My brother and nephew win the match –
3 games to zero. Before leaving, I try to call my brother,
who has disappeared into some weird basement area, on
my cell phone in the lobby, but it's against the rules

to use a cell phone in the lobby. I pass a young couple,
going to the wedding, that looks like a glittering Ralph
Lauren advertisement and I can't believe that this strange,
sexist, misogynist, racist, homophobic, anti-Semitic, elitist
world still exists in any facsimile. I try to practice yoga
and stay calm. I forget to wave farewell to the
guard watching the security cameras, but I ask the

man behind the desk which way to the closest subway
(another broken rule – taking the subway). It's a relief

when I push through the turnstile to enter into the
crowds on a Saturday night, but it's also a shock
to see all the people squashed with so little money
in comparison to the people playing the racquet
games. The families pushing their babies in cheap
strollers onto subway cars after a day of window
shopping or going to Central Park. The teenagers
looking for a little fun or the young couples
chasing romance and a dream in the big city.

SAVAGERY

I had a big steak
at a fancy steak place.

Normally, I don't
eat steak.

But I was with some bankers,
who helped me with a loan,

and they ordered steak
so I ordered steak too.

Turtle soup
was also on the menu,

but I tried not to think about it
because I like turtles.

Thinking about turtle parts
floating in broth

might plunge me into despair,
so I ordered a pear martini instead,

and sipped it while devouring
a piece of cow.

THE TODAY SHOW

There was a bear
eating strawberries
on The Today Show today,
and I really liked
that bear.

He was so big
and brown,
and all he cared
about were those
little red berries.

His whole being
focused on that bowl
in front of him
with the tiny bits
of juicy sweetness.

He didn't care
about Lester Holt
and his sexy good looks, or
the bubbly animal trainer, or
the camera crew, or

Rockefeller Center, or
New York City, or
the millions of people

watching him
eat those berries.

All he cared about
was the food,
and sometimes,
I feel like that
too.

FOUR

A BRIEF HISTORY OF POETRY AND VIOLENCE

I

I wrote some love sonnets
inspired by the love sonnets
of Elizabeth Barrett Browning

and then I read that her family wealth
came from Jamaican sugar plantations

and it occurred to me that
I might know the exact location of
those sugar plantations because
my family also owned a home
in Jamaica.

So I googled "Barrett Sugar
Plantations in Jamaica"
and quickly realized that
Elizabeth's father had probably
been born in the same hills
where my mother's ashes
were sprinkled.

II

They were sprinkled there,
because she loved the view

of those lush green hills
behind her house,
almost more than she loved
the view of the soft blue
Caribbean Sea, stretching out
in the distance in front of it.

It is hard to imagine
the abundance of birds and flowers –
the feathery, purple-pink bougainvillea –
especially against the background of
that soft blue sea or
those lush green hills,
and the circus-colored hibiscus
in yellow, red, and orange with
their lurid pink tongues
reaching out into the world,

almost as obscene as
the bright orange balloons
that blow up on the necks
of the tiny green salamanders
that crawl all over the smooth
palm tree trunks arching
towards the sky, or up and
down the walls of any room
with open windows. I thought
the salamanders were afraid
when I leaned in too close,
and that orange ballooned,
but someone told me that
they were sexually aroused.

Or the strange fruits and vegetables –
the pale green, juicy chou chou
served with chicken and rice for dinner,
and the yellow ackee looking like
scrambled eggs for breakfast,
and the sweetsop with its milky
white sweetness sucked off
shiny black seeds. And

hummingbirds hovering
near flowers
everywhere.

III

It is hard
to imagine
that island.

It is hard
to imagine the history
that happened in
those lush green hills
by the soft blue sea.

The history,
which still happens,
and still
is hard.

IV

One afternoon in the sun,
my mother described her friend,
the wife of a wealthy jeweler
from Philadelphia, being dragged
out of her home near Montego Bay,
by her hair and beaten during
an uprising in the 1960s or '70s.

"What happened to her?"
I asked in horror, disbelief, and
anger at my mother
for buying a house in
such an unsafe place.

"As far as I know,
she still vacations here,"
my mother answered curtly,
as if I was a wimp
and no child of hers –
a familiar response.

Later, we visited one of the nearby sugar plantations,
which had been fixed up as a tourist attraction.
They told the story of Annie Palmer, the White Witch,
who murdered her husbands and was so brutal
to her slaves that they finally rebelled
and murdered her.

We rode horses up past Rose Hall,
where Annie Palmer murdered and
was murdered, and the tour guide
showed us the home of country singer
Johnny Cash, who lived in Cinnamon Hill,
the old Barrett Sugar Plantation.

V

Why did my mother buy a house in Jamaica?
Because her favorite part of the year was
always the vacations she took in the Caribbean.

VI

And I think it all started when she was in boarding school and flew to
Cuba in 1951 with her father and mother and younger sister. They picked
up her boyfriend, who was stationed in the army, near her parents' place
in Florida, and the following day, they all flew to Cuba in the company
propeller plane, which was affectionately called "Penelope." My mother
and her sister played Canasta on a table between them in the plane. Her
father probably had business in Cuba, as he was busy expanding Morton
Salt from a national to an international company.

In Havana, they all sat around a big table at an outdoor restaurant with
Spanish Colonial architecture in the background.

Castro's revolution was less than seven years away.

VII

I never saw my mother read a newspaper.
She only read best-selling fiction by authors such as Danielle Steele, Sidney
Sheldon, and E. L. Doctorow.

"Ignorance is bliss" was one of her favorite expressions,

and another one was, "Whatever turns you on."

I never saw anybody take a vacation like her. Nothing, absolutely nothing,
mattered to her except the deep penetrating rays of the sun. She could lie
all day in the tropical light, when she wasn't stretched out on a lounge
chair in the shade, sipping a drink, and reading her book.

VIII

We're all living off the labor of other people –

some more than others.

IX

Elizabeth Barrett Browning was able to write poems
because of the wealth in her family
from Jamaican sugar plantations,
and my mother could buy a home in Jamaica
because of the wealth in her family

from American corporations –
not just Morton Salt.

Both families got their fingers
into the pie
early on –
so to speak.

Edward Barrett Moulton Barrett, son of Elizabeth Barrett and Charles Moulton, and father to the future poet, had to keep Barrett as his last name in order to inherit the family fortune. He was born on the Cinnamon Hill Plantation in 1785. His family had arrived on the island in 1655, the same year the English conquered the Spanish, who previously colonized the place.

By the middle of the eighteenth century, the Barretts owned 84,000 acres and 2,000 slaves on the island.

The family of the mother of the future poet also owned sugar plantations in the West Indies, as did the family of the future poet's future husband, Robert Browning.

They were all living off the blood of slaves, as Elizabeth Barrett Browning put it.

They also had the blood of slaves coursing through their veins.

Elizabeth believed that the African blood in her family came from the family of her grandfather Charles Moulton, whose father was in command of a war ship stationed in the West Indies, but there is no mention of his mother; so maybe she was the slave who introduced African blood into the Barrett bloodlines.

X

I Googled "biological factors determining race" and Yahoo answered that the concept of race used by the Census Bureau is a sociopolitical construct.

XI

I had a summer romance once with a young man who was of mixed race.

After we left a party one night, he commented, "That party was so white!" and I had no idea what he was talking about.

His father was English. His mother was French. He was educated in Switzerland, but he had been born on Barbados and his grandmother or great-grandmother was Afro-Caribbean.

XII

I also grew up with Elsa, a woman from Trinidad, who lived in a room behind the kitchen and cooked our meals and babysat whenever our mother left the house, which seemed to be often.

After Elsa prepared dinner, my mother had us light candles on the dining room table and turn on some music. She liked to listen to Judy Collins, Harry Belafonte, Frank Sinatra, and Johnny Cash.

XIII

One Christmas, Johnny Cash and his family
were taken hostage at their Cinnamon Hill home
by some Jamaican drug addicts,
who were later captured by police
and died in custody.
The Jamaican government
was very angry
about the bad publicity
and its effect on
the Jamaican tourist industry.
Johnny Cash said
that he felt sorry
for the drug addicts,
as he was a drug addict, too.

Today, the old Barrett plantation house
sits on the edge of the Cinnamon Hill
Golf Course. When I asked my brother,
"Who lives there now?" he answered that
he had asked the same question
a few times but had never gotten
a straight answer.

"Probably a drug lord," I thought
as drugs are such big business
in Jamaica ever since the Soviet Union
collapsed and stopped investing in the
Jamaican economy and recent U.S. policies,

such as NAFTA, decimated
their manufacturing industry.

XIV

In 2010, Jamaica agreed
to a U.S. extradition request
for the Jamaican gang boss
Christopher Coke, and Kingston
was under siege for a month
while police tried to locate
and capture the notorious criminal
who locals regarded as a modern day
Robin Hood. I called my sister,
who was vacationing in Jamaica
at the time, and we joked about
the whereabouts of Christopher Coke.

On March 7, 2012 Prince Harry
danced to Bob Marley in Jamaica
in celebration of the Queen
on her Diamond Jubilee.

And on March 15, 2012, Christopher Coke
appeared for sentencing in a Manhattan court.

XV

Cinnamon Hill was built in 1747.
There was a slave revolt
in 1831 and in 1832
Elizabeth Barrett Browning's father
was forced to sell his rural estate
in England, where Elizabeth grew up,
because he lost money from
the slave revolt and mismanagement
of the sugar plantations in Jamaica.
Elizabeth and her family were afraid
that they would have to move to Jamaica,
but her uncle ran the plantation
until he died in 1837 and then
some of Elizabeth's brothers
were sent overseas
to run the place.

Eventually, the Barretts moved to London,
where Elizabeth began speaking out
against slavery, the poor treatment of women,
and bad working conditions in the factories.
She published a book called "Poems"
in 1844 and received a visit
from a younger poet named
Robert Browning, who admired
both her and her poems.
She wrote her famous love sonnets to him.

XVI

For years, my brother and his wife
have been bringing their children
to the house in Jamaica
near the old Barrett plantation
that they bought from my mother.
I have only been there twice
since my mother died almost
two decades ago, but
there is a sweet woman
named Iona, who used to make
flower arrangements in every room
from all those crazy colors
and obscene flora and my mother,
who loved fresh flowers,
noticed them and promoted her
to the position of cook, where
she has stayed ever since.
She cooks the chou chou
and ackee as well as prepares
all the exotic fruits.
Whenever I call the house
to speak with a vacationing relative,
Iona answers and recognizes
my voice.

"We long to see you!"
she practically wails
into the phone.

SALT GIRLS

When my mother died, I inherited one of her coats. It was a dark, dusty purple ski jacket, which she wore the last winter that she was alive. In the pocket, I found a bunch of small paper packets of Morton Salt. My mother had probably picked up those salt packages in a fast food restaurant during the 1990s, almost one hundred years after her grandfather started working at a salt company. As she was not the hoarding type, my mother stashed those salt packages in her pocket for a reason. I knew they held a special significance for her. They were the same kind of salt packages that were developed over a five-year period in the 1950s when her father was president of Morton Salt. At the time, Morton Salt planned to sell the small salt packages to the airlines for their in-flight food service. My grandfather, who loved to fly airplanes, was always searching for innovative ways to connect business with pleasure. In 1958, just after I was born, my grandmother mentioned the new salt packets in one of her last letters to my mother. She was impressed by how many packets the factory could produce in such a short amount of time. Of course, she did not mention in her letter how depressed she was by the fact that her husband had fallen in love with one of his secretaries.

But putting business aside, there is something very poetic about salt. I have always equated salt with sadness, but historically, people have identified salt with wealth. The Latin root of "salary" comes from "salarium," which was the salt with which Roman legionnaires were paid. Greeks traded slaves for salt. There is something inherently tragic about wealth – especially trading people and their time for things that are not worth as much as the people. In the process, things become worth more than people and people become enslaved to things. And what is that thing called salt? The scientific definition of common salt is a chemical compound of a metal and an acid, otherwise known as sodium chloride. It is a mineral, an inorganic substance occurring naturally in the earth. It is abundant and accessible throughout the world. Salt and water merge instantly. That metal and acid compound disintegrates even if there is moisture in the air. Strange that something so solid dissolves and becomes fluid so easily merging with many different substances as a result. But long after the heat has evaporated the water, salt remains. The salt in the sea comes from the stones at the bottom of it. At some point, human beings crawled out of the sea in an amphibian form and retained salt in their bodies. Salt is in our blood. We can taste it in our tears. We lose it through our sweat. We need it. Salt connects us to the rest of world.

When I found those packages of salt in my mother's pocket, I thought of her fondling them like prayer beads while she was dying. During her illness from cancer and chemotherapy treatments, her second husband, who was not my father, would take her on drives in his truck to get her out of the house. I imagined her looking out the window of his truck at the Pennsylvania countryside in early spring and touching those packets of salt. The feel of those salt packages must have reminded her of the past and provided some solace as she surveyed the rural landscape. Perhaps she remembered her privileged childhood in an urban setting, where her father and grandfather devoted their lives to selling salt while her mother and grandmother concentrated on running various households and attending social affairs. Did she wonder why she was here with a man who drove trucks and worked in construction most of his life? She had done everything in her power to run away from Chicago and create her own life, yet her truck-driver husband and executive father had more in common than most people would imagine. Besides blonde hair and blue eyes, they both loved all forms of transportation and commanded like kings the worlds that surrounded them. But perhaps my mother disoriented from illness, suddenly wondered what had brought her so far from her childhood home and how the elegant surroundings of her youth had disappeared so fast - just as she was about to disappear - like salt dissolving in water.

Humans were so enamored with salt that they set out to harvest it from the sea and extract it from the land. However, before the internal combustion engine and earth moving equipment, mining salt was expensive and dangerous. Mostly slaves and prisoners did the hard work of harvesting salt, hence the phrase "slaving in the salt mines." And because it was so hard to obtain and had so many beneficial qualities besides flavor, salt became very valuable. One of its most powerful qualities was the ability to preserve food. Some historians credit salt with being the foundation of civilization because it freed people from a dependence on seasonal foods. People could travel long distances and survive harsh winters with salted fish, meat, and vegetables. They could harvest food – especially fish – preserve it with salt, sell it, and become rich.

Yet my mother always seemed leery of salt. You could not hand her a shaker of salt. She considered it bad luck to pass the salt without setting it down on the table first. I do not know how many times we were out at a restaurant when she asked me to please pass the salt. I would dutifully grab the container and swing it in her direction. When I stopped mid-air with the shaker, my mother pursed her lips sourly and shook her head. Every time I was surprised by this uncharacteristic tic and thought, "What is your problem? You asked for the salt!" Then I would remember her idiosyncratic superstition, set the salt down on the table, and shake my head in annoyance. She pretended to be so modern in every other way. I was always unnerved by her religious devotion to this one habit, which evoked the dark ages. And there was a connection between my mother's superstition and the dark ages. At that time and before, because of its great value, people suspected bad luck if anyone spilled salt. In da Vinci's painting of "The Last Supper," he depicts an overturned container of salt on the table.

But salt also has healing qualities. It strengthens the blood. It soothes and relieves fatigue. It purifies as an eyewash or mouthwash. It cleans open wounds. Salt is so essential to human life that it is often used as a metaphor for desirable human qualities. The "salt of the earth" are people with a wholesome influence upon society based on the belief that they are more connected to the earth. Salt became a symbol of incorruptibility because of its preservative qualities. In some cultures, people swore on salt rather than a Bible.

If only salt had been healing for my family. If only my relatives had not been so consumed with the business of selling salt. In the process of acquiring huge amounts of salt, they must have spilled a lot of it causing much bad luck. My mother rarely mentioned Morton Salt. Perhaps it was impossible for her to separate the unspeakable tragedies that had occurred in her family from the salt. Her refusal to take that salt from my hand was the only way to express her grief. She had been taught not to complain or brag about her family's good fortune. No one ever admitted that my grandmother had probably killed herself because her husband fell in love with his secretaries. People in my mother's family usually kept quiet and did not ask any unpleasant questions.

Most likely, my mother and her sisters had been excluded from the salt business because they were women. Morton Salt passed out of the family because there was no male heir. All of the cash from the business went to the relatives of the last, surviving secretary, who became my grandfather's wife a few years before he died. My step-grandmother left all of the cash to her blood relatives, and the house and furniture, which came from my grandmother's family anyway, to her husband's descendants. When the descendants of my grandmother and grandfather inherited that white elephant of a house and no cash, there were five employees working there and it had a leaky roof. There had also been a gasoline spill on the property, which was still being cleaned up and had already cost hundreds of thousands of dollars. At the time, I thought that house would sink us to the bottom of the sea, where the problem began in the first place – with all those salty stones.

But how did all this salt business begin? That damned steam engine accelerating everything during the Industrial Revolution – making it so easy and fast to clear the land and mine the salt, plant the seeds, harvest the produce, and fatten the animals. Coal fueling the trains and refrigerated train cars transporting grain, cattle and hogs as food for the rest of the country created a huge demand for salt. Chicago was famous for its meatpacking industry. In 1879, a businessman convinced Joy Morton to invest ten thousand dollars in his salt business, which had always been stable but had greatly increased with the meatpacking trade. Eventually, Joy Morton bought out the businessman's share and founded Joy Morton and Company in 1886. Ten years later, when my great-grandfather was working as a clerk in the Chicago sales office, the company took over Standard Salt Company of Ohio.

I have a copy of a badly typed letter from my great-grandfather to his sister in Aberdeen, Scotland, written in 1898. My great-grandfather was learning shorthand and typing in the hopes of becoming Joy Morton's assistant. The typewriter was one of many new inventions transforming the office environment. Successful businessmen prided themselves on grooming young employees for important positions within the company, and Joy Morton needed an assistant who could type. My great-grandfather wrote to his sister that if he were able to succeed at this job, he would have it made in America. When he had figured out how to "use this confound machine to better advantage," he would go into more detail. In a subsequent letter dated 1900, his typing was greatly improved. He had moved from a boarding house to renting a room in the home of a lawyer and he asked his sister, Janet, to send him her photograph and his sister, Bella, to paint him a picture to decorate his room. In the last decade of his life, during the 1930s, he wrote to one of his buddies from Aberdeen, with whom he had traveled to New York and stayed in boarding houses while looking for work. His buddy had returned to Scotland but my great-grandfather decided to head out west. He told his buddy that he had been made president of Morton Salt.

My grandfather inherited the position of president of the company when his father died in 1941. Growing up, I always heard the rumor that the image of the Morton Salt Girl was taken from a photograph of my grandmother as a little girl.

As the business expanded, Morton Salt needed to sell salt as a household product as well as a commercial one. So in 1914, they put the image of a little girl on the box to make it more appealing to all of those housewives who they wanted as customers. The image had been updated in 1933, four years after my grandparents married, and then again in 1941, and in 1956, when their marriage was falling apart. So I was probably not looking at my grandmother on the saltbox while I was growing up in the 1960s. And then the image changed again in 1968 when I was ten years old. Instead of the cute, curly braids and ruffled dress, the new salt girl had short, straight hair and a short, straight dress. There was a lot less detail in the image. I guess that they were going for the minimalist look. She appeared generic instead - like she was nobody's grandmother.

How many times has that image of the Morton Salt girl been reproduced? How many times has it sold salt? When you reach for that box in a super-market, is it the salt, or the little girl, or the blue, or the combination of all three, which motivates you to buy? Is it the memory of that blue box on your mother's shelf, along with the Kellogg's corn flakes and Pillsbury flour, which makes you buy that particular brand? Such a simple box with such a simple image and such a simple motto, "When it rains, it pours." Such a deceptively easy solution to the problem represented by that downpour of rain pictured on the saltbox – an umbrella and a salt that pours easily when it rains. Morton had discovered a chemical to keep the salt from dissolving too quickly in moist air. Their slogan to sell salt might have started out as a simple advertisement, but it ended up as a description for disaster. People use that expression all the time to describe their troubles and it has nothing to do with salt. Just the other day, I heard a football player on the television use the expression to explain why his team lost the game. "It was a number of factors. You know… when it rains, it pours."

To tell you the truth, it looks very sad to me - the blue, the girl by herself, the rain, and the picture of a box of salt on a box of salt. It is my grandmother alone, my mother alone, myself alone - all of these women deserted for the selling of salt. But it is the image of the lonely, little girl that actually sells the salt.

I visited my step-grandmother at the rotting mansion that she willed to us two years before she died. I knew that my grandfather had left everything to his second wife, perhaps because my mother and her sisters had another source of income from my grandmother's side of the family. I did not know that until my step-grandmother changed my grandfather's will, everything was left to his children and grandchildren upon her death. Perhaps he gave her the option to change his will since that house was such a white elephant and she might need more financial flexibility. But she changed the will almost as soon as she could so that all of the money would go to her nieces and nephews, and all of the liabilities would come to us in the form of that house. Yes, because my mother died, I inherited some money set aside by a wise relative from my grandmother's side of the family, but my cousins from the Morton Salt side of the family, whose parents are still alive, have worked and brought up families with no inheritance. And the oldest male cousin recently died with no money at all.

It was June when a friend and I visited my step-grandmother. We sat out on the back porch overlooking Lake Geneva, Wisconsin. The back porch was elevated on a large pedestal with many steps leading down to the back lawn, which sloped down to the lake. Huge, fluted white columns supported a roof high above the porch. It was one of the most elegant homes on the lake, which was sometimes called the "Newport of the Midwest." My step-grandmother settled back in the porch furniture and eyed my friend and me suspiciously. What did we want? I wanted my friend to take a photograph of the portrait of my grandmother in the dining room because I did not know who would inherit it. I remembered that portrait fondly. It was one of the few images of my grandmother that I saw as I was growing up. It was a large, John Singer Sargent-like painting of her as a young woman holding her dog. She was dressed in a long, black gown with white lace around the collar and short sleeves. There was also a thick sash of white lace wrapped around her waist and knotted at her hip where the rest of it fell to the floor. One arm hung down languorously along side the lace. The other arm held her small dog close to her chest. She stared out defiantly alone – except for the dog.

Perhaps my step-grandmother felt guilty about disinheriting eleven grand-children and expected some sort of confrontation – even though at the time I had no idea that she had disinherited us. I felt no malice towards her because I trusted that my family had been decent to her and that she would be decent in return. I was wrong. But most people would probably identify with a secretary diverting an inheritance from a wealthy family rather than with the children who were robbed of their inheritance. Even though people connected my family with Morton Salt either because they knew the story or had heard some gossip, the truth is that we inherited nothing from Morton Salt.

And it's also possible that the father of my grandmother, eventually heard the rumor that his daughter did not die of a heart attack as had been declared without an autopsy, but that she died of an overdose of pills. Her youngest daughter found her dead in their Chicago penthouse with the empty pill bottles nearby. My grandmother was also found holding a small sculpture she had made of a crying baby, which most of my cousins and I assumed was her suicide note. Before her marriage, my grandmother had studied sculpture in Paris and continued to make art while she was married and raising three children. I know that my great-grandfather re-wrote his will immediately after my grandmother died leaving the bulk of his fortune to her descendants, because I found a copy of that will in my mother's house. However, eventually he re-wrote his will again leaving the bulk of his fortune in control of a much younger second wife.

It is not the loss of money that upsets me. It is the total disempowerment and disregard of the women in my family – marrying them for their money, spending their fortunes, not including them in business, then abandoning them and their children, and finally disinheriting them. The enormous price that has been extracted from the women in my family does not appear in the accounting books. There is no financial reparation that would absolve those misdeeds and everyone who has been involved in them. On top of everything else, no one even recognizes the wrong that has been done. It is so accepted that it is as invisible as salt dissolved in water. Even my family refuses to admit that anything bad has happened. My cousins who are working and raising families without any inheritance, after growing up with a grandfather who lived like a prince, and parents who were also very wealthy, do so with a serenity and humility that I find impressive. They would most likely disapprove of my diatribe.

I want to mourn the deaths of my mother and grandmother with some sort of honesty. A few years after her father died, my mother discovered that she did not have the strength to grow old. Maybe it had something to do with a lack of love. She had tried so hard to please her father, to be the son that he never had, to succeed in business, and fly airplanes. In the end, she even married a man who looked and acted like her father. But she was just a girl and nothing that she did would ever matter in the eyes of the world. She was like the generic young girl on the saltbox – so many of those images of a young girl reproduced and thrown away as many times as they are reproduced.

But maybe I complain too much. Maybe I am more like Lot's wife in the bible, looking back, longing for the good life, as everything falls apart.

The angels warned Lot to take his wife and children out of the city, because the Lord was going to rain down fire and brimstone on that evil place. But they were not supposed to look back as they fled, and Lot's wife did look back, so she turned into a pillar of salt. She hesitated. She took a moment to think, to look back, to reflect, to question what had happened, and what was going to happen. And that was dangerous. What do we know about Lot's wife other than the fact that she was married to Lot? She was disobedient, unlucky, and unknown. She was the original salt girl.

The adjective *salty* means tasting of salt. The verb *to salt* means to season with salt, to preserve in salt, to put aside for the future, as in salt it away. Some salt expressions: salt marsh, *a marsh that is flooded by the sea at high tide*; take it with a grain of salt, *not believe it wholly*; worth one's salt, *competent, deserving one's position*. In the time when Greeks bartered salt for slaves, disappointment in productivity gave rise to the expression that someone was "not worth his salt."

I have a small ranch house near a salt marsh. They used to produce a lot of salt in the area around my house and use it for preserving fish, but now all of the salt businesses are gone. I walk in the salt marsh at low tide in the winter. When the sun evaporates the seawater, only the salt remains. All the water, motion, and life are gone. The mineral is left behind on the sand. That metal and acid compound shimmers in the sun like perpetual snow.

FIVE

YANKEE CANDLE

At my bi-annual check-up, the doctor told me only a few more pounds and I will be officially obese.

I passed the Yankee Candle Factory on the highway by the big Yankee Candle billboard announcing that they have five new scents and showing a tropical scene to advertise their new tropical scent.

By the time I moved out of the city at about 40 years old, I weighed 145 pounds and thought, "I have to lose that extra fifteen pounds."

I can smell the Yankee Candles as my sister and I enter the restaurant. I guess this is Yankee Candle country, but it's early for lunch and mid-week, so the place is empty.

Instead, I gained fifteen more pounds and by the time I moved back to the city almost eight years later, I weighed about 160.

I imagine in less wintry weather, this place is full of Yankee Candle enthusiasts. Who are they and how did Yankee Candles become so popular?

By the time I was fifty, I weighed 175. I went on a trip with someone who said she weighed 200 when she joined Weight Watchers and I agreed that was too much.

I am somewhat surprised that they have two versions of the Reuben sandwich on their menu, as that seems more like New York City food than

Yankee Candle country fare.

But five years later, I weighed 200 pounds. I think it was due to stress and my life being so out of balance.

I order the pastrami version while my sister is excited to get "The Pilgrim," a Thanksgiving feast of turkey, stuffing, cranberry sauce, and gravy in February rather than November – and in Yankee Candle country no less!

I was determined to stay single but being single can cause a lot of stress and then I got into a bad situation where I was being harassed and I was trapped.

We both order a cup of potato broccoli soup and coleslaw rather than fries with our sandwich. I enjoy seeing my sister because we agree on a lot of things, such as our food choices and that the Yankee Candle billboard is a bit extreme.

I must have gained at least 40 pounds because I was fighting for my life and I couldn't digest my food. And yet food was the supreme pleasure in my life.

For dessert, we decide to share a slice of the pecan pie, which comes with a scoop of vanilla ice cream *and* whipped cream. It tastes good with coffee. And those chocolate mints with a layer of green wrapped in foil come with the bill.

WE WERE ONCE DOLPHINS

We were once dolphins swimming
in the same pod – so playful and free!

I was your wife and I died young,
so this is your chance to love me
as an older woman.

You were my son.
I was your mother.
I rejoice at seeing you
so successful, happy, and loved
by so many gorgeous women!

We were sisters. We were brothers.
We were sister and brother,
girlfriend and boyfriend,
girlfriends and boyfriends,

just friends.

We were lovers.

I was your old dog.
You were my young puppy.

You were rich.
I was poor.

One of us was white,
the other dark
like a Moor.

We were so ecstatic
to see each other again
in this lifetime, that we almost
couldn't contain our laughter –
as if we might break loose
from the pod and leap
into the air making sounds
of ridiculous glee! Making sounds
in the air – eee! eee!

FRUIT COBBLER

This fruit cobbler
with whipped cream
and a café latte
are my friends.

I smile
at the woman
at the next table
with a handsome, young
husband or boyfriend.

I have the beautiful
fruit cobbler with
whipped cream, which
I see her eyeing
jealously.

They are tourists.
They have guidebooks.

In a corner booth
by the window,
there's a semi-famous
actor talking frenetically.

At another table,
there's a middle-aged
couple trying to look young

by acting romantic.
On either side of me,
two middle-aged men –
one eating a salad, the other
eating a sausage.

Behind me, there's a family
with a baby and one set
of grandparents, and on
the other side of them
someone is discussing
an art catalogue and
when the sculptures
will arrive. I eat

my fruit cobbler slowly,
wondering when the bill
for my very sheltered,
very privileged life
will come due.
Wondering
if my mother ever
wondered about that –
if there was something
she could do to stave
off disaster, because

you always feel it
knocking at the door,
waiting to come in –
no matter how
seemingly safe
your surroundings.

ATHENA AND PAN

I like when you scowl at me
as if I were some heathen
who needed to be expelled
from the church and I smile
playfully back at you like
a lunatic. You have no idea
what you are up against and
who loves you, but I know
who you are. I love your mortal
ways, your earthiness, how
grounded you are in the day
to day, riding the subway,
observing people, helping them.
I want to protect your innocence,
play the lunatic, guard your love,
guard our love, (guard all love).
Which goddess am I? Maybe
Athena, the smart one, the tough
one, the goddess of war? The one
who wants more, who wants you.
We goddesses like to dress up as
older women because then nobody
pays attention to us and we can
do what we want. But maybe
you are Pan, the goat god,
the wild god of shepherds
and rustic music (heavy metal
and retro tunes in contemporary

terms). You are in disguise too and one day you will surprise and seduce me with music from your flute (or iPod). I will give up my warring ways and virginity, as there will be no need for feminism at that future date. Then we can take our place in the clouds (with soundcloud.com) and be comfortable.

USING YOU

I use you
as a muse.
I am a poet
and I don't want
to blow it
by telling you
that I use you
because then
I might lose you.
(Even though
I don't have you.)
I love you but
I don't show it.
However, I think
you know it.
Is it wrong
to go on so long
without telling you
what's going on?
How I am
amusing myself
by using and
possibly abusing
you as a muse?
Do you see
how confusing
this using
can be?

THE OLD DOG MUST GO

No, the old dog
must not go.
This dog
will stay and eat,
sleep, and even
play, the way
some old dogs
do. He'll go
when he's through
with all the things
there are for old
dogs to do.

And I will
clean up
his messes
and help to
pick him up
from the floor
and run him
to the door
before he sprays
the carpet after
a long night,
during which I run
to the bathroom
at least one time
if not more.

Even the Tarot
Reader said I
have to let him
go. I have to let
him know that
I will be fine
when he goes.
But I think it
is much harder
for him to leave
than for me
to let him go,
because he doesn't
know where he's
going to go
after this
and he likes
being here
with me,
so he keeps
trying to be
a good dog.

He lives
for those treats —
that freeze dried
raw meat and
won't it be sweet
when he finally
lets go
in his own way,

when he finally
lies down and
realizes that it's
too much trouble
to get up, that
he would do it
if he were just
a pup, but he's
not. And won't it
be sweet when he
closes his eyes and
realizes how much
I love him,
that it's even okay
if he dies.

CAFÉ SABARSKY

I am sitting in Café Sabarsky
drinking coffee with schlag.
Schlag means whipped cream
and if there's one word to know
in German, it's schlag, because
this coffee is good.

I have a corner, cushioned seat
with a view of Central Park outside
the big windows. The yellow leaves
swirl against a strong blue sky. In
this dark, wood-paneled room
I could just as well be in Vienna

sipping coffee with schlag in
an earlier century. I could just
as well be Sigmund Freud or
Virginia Woolf. I have just had
my first poem published and
it is about Virginia Woolf.

She is here in this room
looking out the windows
at the swirling yellow leaves.

She is sipping coffee, sitting
alone with her thoughts. *How
much better is silence, the coffee*

*cup, the table. How much better
to sit by myself like the solitary
seabird on the stake that opens
its wings. Let me sit here forever
with bare things, this coffee cup,
this knife, this fork, things in*

themselves, myself being myself.
Let me sit here forever.

CONGRATULATE YOURSELF

Because there are things that you promised yourself as a child that you would do as an adult and you did them.

Like today I looked up from reading a book by Adrienne Rich on the beach, and there was this great expanse of ocean and sky in front of me that looked like a painting of the horizon by Pat de Groot.

The water was dark and the sky was light with thin wisps of white.

There was a seagull flying above, then two, and they made me realize that the whole thing was three-dimensional.

All that ocean and sky looked like God and I remembered that I had always promised myself as a child that I would live near the beach.

I also wanted to have a lot of animals. I wanted to be a hermit. I wanted to be a monk. I wanted to live simply. I wanted to be an actor, but not a famous one.

(Recently, I read a quote equating acting and the church via the idea that someone is watching and every action has a purpose and meaning – and I realized that I am more devout than I thought.)

I never wanted to get married.

I never wanted to have a child.

I promised myself that I would not bring another sensitive soul into this senseless set-up and then have no answer for them when they asked me why.

It would be better for the planet and all the other animals living on a planet overrun by human beings if I didn't have children.

I also wanted to save the planet, but I was pretty sure that wasn't going to happen.

I wanted to live without lying.

I wanted to live without hurting other people.

In many ways I failed,

but I did manage to live by the beach for a while and have a dog.

SEPTEMBER 22, 2014

I wake up and turn on
the television – 3 Afghan
soldiers have escaped from
the mall in Hyannis, where I
will be going later in the day.
By then, they will have been
captured trying to cross
the Canadian border near
Niagara Falls – between
now and then, here and
there, AM and PM, me
and them. They were
training at a military
base on Cape Cod.

The exterminator arrives
to get rid of the bees.
My friend found them
while trying to clean
the rain gutters. I take
the dead bees in a bag
to the dump. Then I call
the doctor's office to try
and schedule a colonoscopy.
I actually get through to
an intelligent human being,
who realizes that I need

the colonoscopy, and
schedules an emergency
appointment with the
physician's assistant.

I call my sister, who
recommended the doctor
and offered to pick me
up after the procedure.
Each day – a string of
pearls – dirty rain
gutters, a friend
cleaning them, bees,
an exterminator, the
dump, a colonoscopy,
sister, lunch, car
tune-up near the Cape
Cod Mall, where 3
Afghans escaped
earlier – running for
their lives or looking
for better ones, as they
said on television.

An embarrassment of
riches in this country,
too much stuff in that
mall – in all malls –
get me out of here
now, take me to the
Canadian border. It

must be better over
there. The people
are nicer anyway.

Wandering around
Hyannis while they
rotate the tires on
my car – a tropical
smoothie with bee
pollen for extra energy
and George Sands'
abbreviated autobiography
purchased at Tim's Used
Books on Main Street.

Then back to that crazy
car dealership where no
story is straight and we
have grown old together.
Drive home to email and
tending to my garden of
friends – Jack's birthday
and book signing party
at Soho House, Mudfish
workshop, Brooklyn Poets
open reading on Columbus
Day. See string of pearls
on Antiques Road Show
just before bed.

Take me to the Canadian
border, to the Canadian

wilderness (not to the
interrogation room where
they took those 3 Afghans).
Free me from the guilt of
all the pain and suffering
I have never known –
what those Afghan soldiers
were running from, of living
in a country that drops bombs
on impoverished nations and people.
Take me to the land of my
dreams for a brief respite
from this dream-like land.

ACKNOWLEDGMENTS

Many thanks to the editors of the following journals for first publishing these poems:

The Straddler: "On Overcoming Obstacles"

WSQ (Women's Studies Quarterly): "One Suicide Engages With Another"

Mudfish: "The Sewers of Paris," "Walking Back," "Reading: The Story of My Childhood"

PMS (poemmemoirstory): "Anti-Postcards"

Washington Square Review: "The Today Show"

And gratitude to Kathleen Ossip, Vijay Seshadri, Fred Marchant, Priscilla Becker, Patricia Carlin, Daisy Fried, Alan Shapiro, Cynthia Huntington, Jill Hoffman and the Mudfish workshop, and Emily Blair for reading and giving important feedback on many of these poems. Thanks also to Peter Davis, Greg and Ron, JB for essential guidance, my sister for technical assistance, and all the other friends and family who have been supportive along the way. But extra gratitude to Jill Hoffman and Box Turtle Press for making the dream of a book come true.

Note: Italics in "Café Sabarsky" are quoted from <u>The Waves</u> by Virginia Woolf

About the Author:

Dell Lemmon received a BFA in acting from Boston University ad then spent two years studying mime in Paris with Etienne Decroux. Later, she earned an MA and Ph.D. in Performance Studies from New York University, where she won an award for her dissertation on Michael Fried's theories of theatricality and the contemporary visual arts. Her poetry has appeared in journals such as *The Straddler, WSQ, Mudfish, PMS (poem-memoirstory),* and *Washington Square Review.* She has read her poems at Poetry Project's New Year's Day Marathon, KGB Bar, Brooklyn Poets, and the Fine Arts Work Center in Provincetown. She lives in Brooklyn and her poems will soon appear in the inaugural volume of *The Brooklyn Poets Anthology* published by Brooklyn Arts Press.

MUDFISH INDIVIDUAL POET SERIES

#1 *Dementia Pugilistica*, David Lawrence

#2 *Black Diaries*, Jill Hoffman

#3 *Too Too Flesh*, Doug Dorph

#4 *Skunk Cabbage*, Harry Waitzman

#5 *Husk*, Terry Phelan

#6 *Marbles*, Mary du Passage

#7 *Fires in Sonoma*, Terry Phelan

#8 *Rending the Garment*, Willa Schneberg

#9 *Vilnius Diary*, Anna Halberstadt

#10 *Single Woman*, Dell Lemmon

Box Turtle Press/Attitude Art Inc.
184 Franklin Street
New York, New York 10013